Deception

RESOURCES FOR BIBLICAL LIVING

Lou Priolo, series editor

Deception

Letting Go of Lying

LOU PRIOLO

PUBLISHING
P.O. BOX 817 • PHILLIPSBURG • NEW JERSEY 08865-0817

Unless otherwise indicated, Scripture quotations are from the NEW AMERICAN STANDARD BIBLE®. Copyright © 1960, 1962, 1963, 1968, 1971, 1972, 1973, 1975, 1977, 1995 by The Lockman Foundation. Used by permission.

Italics within Scripture quotations indicate emphasis added.

Printed in the United States of America

Library of Congress Cataloging-in-Publication Data

Priolo, Lou.
  Deception : letting go of lying / Lou Priolo.
    p. cm. — (Resources for biblical living)
  Includes bibliographical references.
  ISBN 978-1-59638-129-2 (pbk.)
  1. Truthfulness and falsehood—Religious aspects—Christianity.
  2. Truthfulness and falsehood—Biblical teaching. I. Title.
  BV4627.F3P75 2008
  177'.3—dc22
                          2008031796

IN 1988, a survey published in the *San Francisco Chronicle* indicated that the average adult lies (or is willing to admit that he lies) 13 times per week. More recent estimates place the frequency from between 20 and 200 lies *per day*. It has been suggested that the two biggest American lies are: "I'm from the government, and I'm here to help you," and "The check is in the mail."

Syndicated columnist Ann Landers once asked her readers to send her their ideas for the third biggest lie. Here is a sample of the responses she received.

- "It's delicious, but I can't eat another bite."
- "So glad you dropped by. I wasn't doing a thing."
- "You don't look a day over forty."
- "The baby is just beautiful."
- "It's a good thing you came in today. We have only two more in stock."
- "Put the map away. I know exactly how to get there."

If you are like most people, you have struggled with telling the truth. As a Christian, this presents a particular problem for you because you not only *know* the truth, but you are *commanded to speak* the truth (in love). The ninth commandment—"You shall not bear false witness against your neighbor"—is one of the most basic biblical directives for living the Christian life (see Ex. 20:16).

"Now wait just one minute! Are you calling me a liar?"

Of course, I don't know how much you actually struggle with lying. But with your permission, I will presume that if you are reading this booklet, you (or someone you love) have a pattern of mishandling the truth.

Perhaps you've tried to change and failed repeatedly—especially in the crunch when the pressure was on. But I have good news for you. You are not alone. Many people of God have struggled with this sin. The Bible is filled with examples of people who have lied. Even well-respected people like Abraham, Jacob, Aaron, David, and the apostle Peter lied under pressure.

Even if you are not a practicing liar, deceit is in your heart. Indeed, "The heart is deceitful above all things . . . who can know it?" (Jer. 17:9 NKJV). David said, "The wicked are estranged from the womb; they go astray from birth, speaking lies" (Ps. 58:3 ESV).

Look at what Paul says in Romans 3:9–13.

> What then? Are we better than they? Not at all; for we have already charged that both Jews and Greeks are all under sin; as it is written,
>
> > "There is none righteous, not even one;
> > There is none who understands,
> > There is none who seeks for God;
> > All have turned aside, together they have become
> > > useless;
> > There is none who does good,
> > There is not even one."
> > "Their throat is an open grave, *With their tongues
> > > they keep deceiving*,"
> > "The poison of asps is under their lips."

Who is Paul talking about here? He's talking about unregenerate man—you and me before we were saved.

Now, some people claim that they never lie. But think about what such people say when they make this assertion. They claim that they never break the ninth commandment. Consider the answer to question 112 of the historic Heidelberg catechism.

Question 112. What is required in the ninth commandment?

6

Answer. That I bear false witness against no man, wrest no one's words; that I be no backbiter [that is, to speak spitefully about someone], or slanderer; that I do not judge, or join in condemning any man rashly, or unheard [that is, without hearing his side of the story]; but that I avoid all sorts of lies and deceit, as the proper works of the devil, unless I would bring down upon myself the heavy wrath of God; likewise, that in judicial and all other dealings I love the truth, speak it uprightly and confess it; and that, as much as I am able, I *defend and promote the honor and reputation* of my neighbor.

Who can really maintain that he never breaks this commandment? To make such a claim is to instantly break it.

A Biblical View of Deception

Have you ever really thought about your dishonesty from God's perspective? You will not change until you do. "Lying lips are an abomination to the Lord, but those who deal faithfully are His delight" (Prov. 12:22).

"Our truth-telling, promise-keeping God who 'cannot lie' takes this business of deception seriously! He *hates* lying! Do you?"[1]

Lying is something that it is *good to hate*:

A righteous man *hates* falsehood. (Prov. 13:5)

I *hate* and *despise* falsehood, but I love Your law. (Ps. 119:163)

Have you ever stopped to identify your own specific *style* of lying? Do you know what tactics you use to keep others from knowing the truth about you? Allow me to help you.

Let's begin looking at the general categories of deception, and then we'll move on to some of the more specific *misleading maneuvers* identified in the Bible. Hopefully, by the time we're

1. J. I. Packer, *Growing in Christ* (Wheaton, IL: Crossway, 1996).

7

through, you will have a pretty good handle on the forms of deception you are most tempted to utilize.

Defining deception is not an easy task. For centuries, people have tried to describe this term. Even theologians do not always agree on every point in this discussion. But there are a couple of points upon which most people agree.

- Deception involves *deliberately* communicating to another person something that one does not believe to be true. (The dictionary defines the verb *lie* as "to make an untrue statement with intent to deceive.") So, when you *intentionally* express something *outwardly* that contradicts that which you judge to be true *inwardly*, you are deceiving.
- Deception is *deliberately* misleading another who has neither been informed of one's intentions to mislead him nor requested to be misled (as in the case of actors, illusionists, football players, etc., whose performances and actions are by their very nature intentionally misleading).

There are two basic ways to deceive. Deception can be accomplished by falsifying information or by concealing information. *Falsification* involves distorting the truth (*changing* the essential facts of a matter). *Concealment* involves withholding vital elements of the truth (*omitting* the essential facts). This is why when American citizens are sworn in before taking the witness stand, they are enjoined *not only* to tell the truth, but to tell the *whole truth* and *nothing but the truth*. These three pledges cover just about every form (and combination) of lying—except possibly *inference* or *insinuation* (which, I suppose, has been omitted from the oath for the benefit of the lawyers).

Now, we're ready to put on our biblical spectacles and take a closer look at a few of the many kinds of lying identified in Scripture. I know of over two dozen different kinds of lies identified in the Bible. I'm sure there are many more.

Think about the enormous breadth and scope of this ilk. There are dozens of kinds (species) of lies (not dozens of lies but dozens of varieties of lies—almost every variety making numerous appearances in Scripture). How familiar are you with each variety? I don't have enough space in this booklet to thoroughly unpack all twenty-three species I have found, but I would like to cover (or should I say "uncover") some of them.

An Outright Lie (or a Direct Untruth)

Let's take a look at the oldest trick in the book. It is found in Genesis 3:1–4.

> Now the serpent was more crafty than any beast of the field which the LORD God had made. And he said to the woman, "Indeed, has God said, 'You shall not eat from any tree of the garden'?" The woman said to the serpent, "From the fruit of the trees of the garden we may eat; but from the fruit of the tree which is in the middle of the garden, God has said, 'You shall not eat from it or touch it, or you will die.'" The serpent said to the woman, *"You surely will not die!"*

Satan verbally negated God's promise. God pledges, "In the day you eat from it, *you shall surely die.*" Now, I know of two ways to interpret Satan's contradiction. Both of them are lies. Either he is playing off the word *surely*, questioning the certainty of God's promise—"You shall not *surely* die—I wouldn't be so *sure* of this dying deal that God has offered you"—or he is using the assertiveness of the word *sure* to oppose and even mock God—"You *surely* (most certainly) will not die!"

Inference (Insinuation)

Let's look at the next verse (Gen. 3:5).

> For God knows that in the day you eat from it *your eyes will be opened, and you will be like God, knowing good and evil.*

What Satan is trying to do here is to cast doubt over God's character (and His motives). The implication is that God is being jealous—in a selfish sort of way. "God is keeping something very special from you. He is omniscient—He has this special knowledge—and He doesn't want to share it with you!"

Satan actually begins his insinuation back in *verse one*: "Indeed, has God said, 'You shall not eat from *any* tree of the garden'?" If you look closely, you can see that he changes the meaning of what God has said by focusing on God's *narrow* prohibition rather than His *broad* concession. Let's look at chapter 2, verses 16-17.

> The LORD God commanded the man, saying, "From *any* tree of the garden *you may eat freely*; but from the tree of the knowledge of good and evil *you shall not eat*, for in the day that you eat from it you will surely die."

By minimizing the concession and maximizing the exemption, Satan twisted the intent of God's condition for Eve's blessing. All he had to do to deceive her with insinuation was to put the emp*ha*sis on the wrong syl*la*ble.

Suppose you and I had been invited to the same social function last Saturday. Then in church on Sunday, your name came up in a conversation I was having with one of our mutual acquaintances. What would you think of me if I announced to him and a few others who were listening, "I spent several hours with him/her yesterday, and he/she was sober the entire time"?

"I would think you were slandering me."

Slandering you? Why? Did I not say something that was fundamentally good about you? Did I not speak the truth?

"Yes, but the inference you made was that I normally am a drunk."

Exactly!

I picked on lawyers a moment ago, but the truth is, if I weren't in the ministry I would probably be an attorney. In fact, I actually was a lawyer in high school. I believe it was the fall of

1971. One of my schoolmates decided to cut our business law class. The teacher gave him the choice of either taking a trip to the principal's office or being placed on trial before his fellow classmates. He chose the latter.

The teacher was to serve as the judge. The class was the jury. One of my fellow classmates was to serve as the defendant's attorney. And, yours truly was appointed as the prosecutor.

On the day of the trial, the evidence was presented, and the defendant took the stand. The conversation that ensued went something like this.

"Why is it that you were not in class on the day in question, Mr. Jones?"

"Because, I had to work."

"And please tell us where you work, Mr. Jones."

"I work at McDonald's."

"So your testimony is that on the day you missed class, you were working at McDonald's. Is that right?"

"That's right."

"Well, suppose I were to tell you that I spoke to your boss this morning, and he told me that you did *not* work during school hours that day?"

At this point my friend (former friend) confessed to the crime.

Then, I turned to the teacher and said, "If it please the court, I really didn't speak to the defendant's boss at MacDonald's. But, I didn't really lie. I simply asked him to 'suppose' that I had spoken to his boss."[2]

The teacher covered his face with his hands and began to shake his head. And that was the end of my legal career!

Concealment

Again, concealment involves withholding essential elements of the truth from those who have a need to know them.

2. I learned this ploy from watching an old Perry Mason episode on television.

Before the fall, Satan concealed a very significant piece of information from Adam and Eve. Do you know what it was?

> "For God knows that in the day you eat from it *your eyes will be opened, and you will be like God, knowing good and evil.*" When the woman saw that the tree was good for food, and that it was a delight to the eyes, and that the tree was desirable to make one wise, she took from its fruit and ate; and she gave also to her husband with her, and he ate. *Then the eyes of both of them were opened, and they knew that they were naked.* (Gen. 3:5–7a)

He told them that their *eyes would be opened* (which they were), and that they would be *like God*, knowing good and evil (which is what happened—sort of). Their eyes were indeed opened, and they did indeed come to know the difference between good and evil. But unlike God (and this is what the serpent neglected to tell them), Adam and Eve would know evil *experientially*. God indeed knows the difference between the two, but His knowledge of evil is not firsthand—but, as it were, from a distance.

Of course, Satan also concealed the sinful and utterly miserable condition that this "new state of enlightenment" would bestow upon them.

Proverbs 10:18 says, "He who *conceals* hatred *has lying lips.*" Solomon equated concealment with lying.

Concealment is often a particular problem for children and young people. There is certain information that parents have a biblical right (if not need) to know about their children's lives. To deliberately keep such information from them is to be less than honest.

I often tell young people: "Your folks are your shepherds—right? More than your friends or your elders, they have the responsibility to teach you not only how to *act like* a Christian, but how to *think and be motivated* like one as well. In order to do that, they are going to have to ask you questions—sometimes very personal ones! And you are obligated to open your hearts to them to give them the information they need to do what God has commanded them to do (see 2 Cor. 6:12–13). When you conceal from them the information they need to bring you up in the discipline and instruction of the Lord, you are sinning *big time!*"

As an avid fisherman, I know a little bit about concealment. One of the most basic rules of fishing has to do with concealment: *Present the bait. Hide the hook!*

Blame-Shifting

Moving down to verse 11 of Genesis 3, we observe yet another form of deception.

> And He said, "Who told you that you were naked? Have you eaten from the tree of which I commanded you not to eat?" The man said, "*The woman whom You gave to be with me, she gave me from the tree, and I ate.*" Then the LORD God said to the woman, "What is this you have done?" And the woman said, "*The serpent deceived me, and I ate.*" (Gen. 3:11–13)

When you try to shift the blame for your own sin, you are practicing deception. To the extent that you attempt to dodge your own culpability by fallaciously shifting the blame from yourself to another, you are being dishonest.

Here are a few familiar examples of blame-shifting:

- "I wouldn't get *angry* at my wife if she wouldn't *nag* me all the time."
- "I wouldn't have been *rebellious* if my husband weren't so *tyrannical.*"
- "I only *snuck out* because Dad doesn't give me enough *freedom.*"
- "I wouldn't *lie* to my parents if they weren't so *distrustful* of me."[3]

3. The irony of this line is that nothing destroys trust as quickly and thoroughly as lying!

The Bible starts with these lies but catalogs a whole lot more. Let's take a look at a few of them.

The "I Don't Know" Lie

> "Then the LORD said to Cain, 'Where is Abel your brother?' And he said, '*I do not know.* Am I my brother's keeper?'" (Gen. 4:9)

Do you remember the story of Rahab the harlot? She apparently had a preference for this particular maneuver for she used it twice in the same deception.[4]

> The king of Jericho sent word to Rahab, saying, "Bring out the men who have come to you, who have entered your house, for they have come to search out all the land." But the woman had taken the two men and hidden them, and she said, "Yes, the men came to me, but I did not know where they were from. It came about when it was time to shut the gate at dark, that the men went out; I do not know where the men went. Pursue them quickly, for you will overtake them." (Josh. 2:3–5)

The religious leaders of Christ's day also resorted to this form of subterfuge.

> When He entered the temple, the chief priests and the elders of the people came to Him while He was teaching, and said, "By what authority are You doing these things, and who gave You this authority?" Jesus said to them, "I will also ask you one thing, which if you tell Me, I will also tell you by what authority I do these things. The baptism of John was from what source, from heaven or from men?" And they began

4. This account often raises the question as to whether it is *always* a sin to lie—especially since Rahab is commended for her faith related to this act in Heb. 11:31. Many see no exception to the immorality of deceit. Some would hold that although lying is overwhelmingly viewed in the Bible as sinful, there may be exceptional occasions (such as in times of war) when it may not be.

reasoning among themselves, saying, "If we say, 'From heaven,' He will say to us, 'Then why did you not believe him?' But if we say, 'From men,' we fear the people; for they all regard John as a prophet." And answering Jesus, they said, *"We do not know."* He also said to them, "Neither will I tell you by what authority I do these things." (Matt. 21:23–27)

The chief priests and elders didn't really accept John as a prophet, but the people who were present did. So, a truthful answer would have been, "We don't believe John's baptism was from God but from men." But being the cowards that they were, they lied.

How many times have parents heard, "I didn't know that" or "I didn't remember your saying that"? That usually doesn't work around my house.

Why? My family has been taught that there are certain things about which they have a biblical responsibility to know and remember:

- What the Bible says about . . . this, that, or the other.
- What the house rules are.
- What their conduct should be as Christians.

In other words, there are some things in life that we are obligated to know. And as soon as we recognize our ignorance in these areas, we are obligated to seek and acquire the knowledge that we lack.

Making Commitments with No Intention of Keeping Them

Like clouds and wind without rain is a man who boasts of gifts he does not give. (Prov. 25:14 NIV)[5]

5. For a biblical example of this variety of deception, see Gen. 34:1–17.

When you make a promise as a Christian, you are biblically obligated[6] to fulfill if, even if it hurts to do so. "[He] who swears to his own hurt and does not change . . . shall never be moved" (Ps. 15:4–5 ESV).[7]

Here are a few common examples:

Child to parent:	"I'll do it tomorrow."
	"I'll pay you back as soon as I get my allowance."
Parent to child:	"If you do that again, I'm going to spank you."
	[Then, after the child does it a second time . . .]
	"I told you if you do that again, I'm going to spank you."
	[The child does it yet again . . .]
	"Don't make me tell you that again!"
Husband to wife:	"We'll go on a date next week."
	"I'll fix it this weekend."
	"We'll talk about it when I get home from work."
	"I'll call you first chance I get."
Wife to husband:	"I'll go on a diet after the holidays."
	"I'll take it back next time I go to the mall."
	"I won't spend more than $50 for that widget."
Employer to employee:	"We can't afford to pay you much right now, but if you 'hang in there' with us, as our company grows, we'll reward your faithfulness."

6. There are, in certain circumstances, honorable ways to *attempt* to break a commitment one has made foolishly (cf. Num. 30:3–15; Prov. 6:1–5).

7. It should also be noted that when a promise is made with every intention of keeping it but is broken without biblical justification, the sin associated with the "broken promise" falls more along the lines of *unfaithfulness* than *deceit*.

Slandering or Talebearing

Take a look at Leviticus 19:16 rendered in two popular English translations.

> You shall not go about as a *slanderer* among your people. (NASB)
> You shall not go about as a *talebearer* among your people. (NKJV)

The words *slanderer* and *talebearer* are used to translate the same Hebrew term. To slander someone is to invent or repeat a lie about him with malicious intent.[8]

Talebearing is to float or repeat a rumor without carefully investigating whether the rumor is factual.

> For lack of wood the fire goes out, and where there is no whisperer [KJV: talebearer], contention quiets down. (Prov. 26:20)

> The words of a talebearer are like tasty trifles, and they go down into the inmost body. (Prov. 18:8 NKJV)

Have you ever done this? You hear something about someone secondhand. You don't know that it is true, but it seems to be in keeping with the person's character—so you repeat it to another as if it *were* or *might be* true. That's talebearing.

Slander is usually the result of faulty information. Many of the facts are either missing or distorted.

As you may know, the first four of the ten commandments show us how to love God—the remaining six how to love our neighbor. The ninth commandment is intended to *guard against* defamation of character. It is meant to *protect* the reputation of our neighbors.

The Bible has much to say about the value of a good reputation.

> A *good* name is to be more desired than great wealth. (Prov. 22:1)

8. The legal definition of slander is "a false defamation that injures the character or reputation of the person defamed."

A *good* name is better than a good ointment. (Eccl. 7:1)

The overseer must be *above reproach*. (Titus 1:7; cf. 1 Tim. 3:2)

We have a vital responsibility to watch out for and protect the good reputation of *others*. That's what love does—it rejoices in the truth!

Have you ever heard of the sin of detraction? It's an archaic term meaning to *speak ill of* or *belittle* someone. The idea behind the word is that of taking away from or reducing the value of something. When you slander someone, you are taking away from (*stealing*, if you please) the honor and good reputation of that person. You are reducing the value of his good name. This is one of the most hurtful things you can do to another. You know how much it hurts because it's been done to you—probably more than once!

We've only just scratched the surface of the different kinds of lies identified in the Bible. While I cannot develop the other lies to which I alluded at the beginning, I have put together a table that will at least begin to familiarize you with most of them.

Type of Deception	Scripture	Explanation/Examples
Hidden Agenda	Judges 3:16–23 Matthew 2:8	A hidden agenda is an ulterior motive (beyond the acceptable motive which has been expressed). Here are some of the hidden agendas people sometimes have when they come to see me for counseling: "I want you to fix my spouse or child." "I want you to help me divorce my husband." "I want custody of my children, and I want you to collect enough evidence to prove (in court) that my wife is an unfit mother." "I want you to sympathize with my self-pity and confirm that I am, in fact, a victim of an illness or of what others have done to me." "I want you to convince my wife not to leave me." "I want you to remove my pain and guilt without my having to change."

Type of Deception	Scripture	Explanation/Examples
Perjury	Malachi 3:5 Matthew 26:59 Mark 14:56–59	Perjury is the deliberate, willful giving of false, misleading, or incomplete testimony under oath. "They [Stephen's opponents from the so-called "Synagogue of the Freed Men"] put forward false witnesses who said, 'This man incessantly speaks against this holy place and the Law; for we have heard him say that this Nazarene, Jesus, will destroy this place and alter the customs which Moses handed down to us'" (Acts 6:13–14).
Fabrication	Exodus 32:21–24	A fabrication is a concocted story assembled for the purpose of deceiving someone. When an individual consistently has "unusual" or "incredible" explanations for his behavior, chances are good he is fabricating. "The reason I was late for class is that I squeezed my toothpaste too hard, and it took me a long time to get it all back into the tube!"
Flattery	Proverbs 5:3; 6:24; 7:5, 21; 28:23; 29:5 Romans 16:18	Flattery is trying to influence or gain an advantage over someone by praising (or pleasing) him above and beyond that which his character merits. It is often a cunning and deceitful kind of praise intended to trap and hurt the unsuspecting and to benefit the one who laid it.* "All the commissioners of the kingdom, the prefects and the satraps, the high officials and the governors have consulted together that the king should establish a statute and enforce an injunction that anyone who makes a petition to any god or man besides you, O king, for thirty days, shall be cast into the lions' den" (Dan. 6:7).
Verbalizing Suspicions or False Conclusions (Beguilement)	1 Samuel 22:11–15	To beguile is to deceive by guile. When unsubstantiated suspicions are verbalized to others, seeds of doubt and distrust can be planted—especially in naive and unsuspecting minds. "My mother doesn't want me to have any fun." "I can just feel it. My husband has been unfaithful to me." "You believe my wife's side of the story rather than mine."

* I have written more extensively about flattery in *Pleasing People: How Not to Be an "Approval Junkie"* (Phillipsburg, NJ: P&R Publishing, 2007).

Type of Deception	Scripture	Explanation/Examples
Diversion	Genesis 4:9 John 4:17–19	A diversion is a clever maneuver intended to draw the attention of its victim away from the issue at hand. Pastor: "Is what your wife is saying about your response to her true?" Parishioner: "Ask her to tell you what she said to me last night."
Partial Truth	Genesis 20:1–12	A partial truth is a form of concealment that discloses a fair portion of truth but purposely omits relevant information that would change the entire completion of the message. Sales manager: "Are you romantically involved with that client?" Salesman: "I did take her to lunch. We're old friends."
Exaggeration	Acts 5:1–11 Numbers 13:30–33	"My mother never lets me have any fun!" "My husband is never home in the evenings before 9:30 or 10:00." Hyperboles can be not only humorous but also defamatory: "My wife has a black belt in shopping."
Covering Up Past Sins	2 Samuel 11:1–12:9 Psalm 32:3–5 Genesis 37:29–35	"Oh, I used to have a little problem with my drinking, but it's under control now." "I don't remember ever being physical with her. A couple of times, I may have pushed her away in self defense; that's all."
Kidding, Teasing, and Joking	Proverbs 26:18–19	"I was only kidding when I threatened to buy my wife that muzzle for her birthday." "I didn't mean it when I called my son a . . . ." "I was only bluffing when I pointed the shotgun at my daughter's boyfriend."

Type of Deception	Scripture	Explanation/Examples
Voice and Body Language Lies	Proverbs 6:12–19	There are a variety of verbal and involuntary nonverbal signals that people send to people who are trained to spot them. When an individual, for example, is evasive—does not directly answer a question, or carefully weighs each word that he utters, or when he appears anxious and excessively nervous, or lets something slip out of his mouth that does not "jibe" (fit) with other things he has said; when he frequently uses vocalized pauses or repeats the same words, or changes the pitch of his voice in response to a question; when he uses fewer gestures than normal in response to your question, he may be lying. Some of the more common nonverbal cues are changes in breathing pattern, changes in the frequency of swallowing, changes in the amount of perspiration, changes in facial color (blushing and blanching), changes in pupil dilation, or frequency of blinking.*
Claiming to Be Close to God while Continuing to Sin	1 John 1:6 1 John 2:4	"God understands that I have no choice but to divorce my husband. I still love God; I just don't love my husband anymore."
Giving the Appearance of One Emotion to Cover Up the Existence of Another Emotion	Matthew 26:69–75	Perhaps the most common and easiest emotion to fake in an attempt to "cover up" how one really feels is anger. Sorrow, fear, and happiness (laughter) are also commonly counterfeited to disguise genuine emotions.
Planting/ Fabricating Evidence	Genesis 37:29–35	A woman presents a dated sales receipt (which she "borrowed" from a friend) to "prove" to her husband that she was in one place, when in fact she was in some other place having a secret rendezvous with another man.

* Paul Ekman, *Telling Lies* (New York: Berkley, 1986), 80–161; Gini Graham Scott, *The Truth About Lying* (Petaluma, CA: Smart Publications, 1994), 175–88.

Type of Deception	Scripture	Explanation/Examples
Acting (e.g., Pretending to Be Crazy)	1 Samuel 21:13–14	An accident victim pretends to be greatly injured so he can collect disability insurance.
	2 Samuel 13:3–6	A psychiatrist's patient pretends to be anxious to continue receiving the controlled substance to which she is addicted.
		A teenager plays the part of the psychological label ("disorder") that his psychologist (for insurance purposes) ascribed to him in order to avoid having to repent of sinful thoughts and/or activities.

The table above is not exhaustive. But the truth is, you and I have told more of these lies than the number of hairs on our heads. Nevertheless, where sin abounds, *grace super abounds* (cf. Rom. 5:20).

Guidelines for Becoming a Teller of the Truth

Now that you have a better understanding of what God thinks of lying and a basic understanding of the breadth and scope of this sin, let's take a look at some things you can do to cooperate with the Spirit's transforming work of grace in your life.

Examine Your Life for Evidences of Regeneration

Habitual lying may be an indication that you don't really know Christ.

> But for the cowardly and unbelieving and abominable and murderers and immoral persons and sorcerers and idolaters and *all liars*, their part will be in the lake that burns with fire and brimstone, which is the second death. (Rev. 21:8)

If you are an *habitual* liar, you ought to be concerned about the implications of this passage on your future. If you lie on a regular basis, you are imitating not the Father in heaven but the "father of lies"—you are not bearing God's image but Satan's.

Look also at what Jesus says in John 8:44.

> *You are of your father the devil,* and you want to do the desires of your father. He was a murderer from the beginning, and does not stand in the truth because there is no truth in him. Whenever he speaks a lie, he speaks from his own nature, for he is a liar and the father of lies.

Richard Baxter gave a somber warning to those who habitually lie.

> Fear God more than man if you would not be liars! The excessive fear of man is a common cause of lying. It is what makes children so apt to lie, to escape the rod, and puts most people, who are overly sensitive to being hurt, in danger of lying in order to avoid the displeasure of others. But why do you not fear God more? His displeasure is unspeakably more terrible! Your parents or master will be angry, and threaten to correct you; but God threatens to damn you—and *His* wrath is a consuming fire! No man's displeasure can reach your souls, and extend into eternity. Will you run into hell to escape punishment on earth? Remember, whenever you are tempted to escape any danger by a lie, that you run a thousand fold greater danger, and that no hurt that you escape by a lie, can possibly be half so great as the hurt it causes. It is as foolish a course as to cure the toothache by cutting off the head![9]

As Luther taught us, we are saved by "faith alone" in the substitutionary death of Christ on the cross, but not by the "faith that is alone." In other words, saving faith will produce a certain amount of substantiating evidence (fruit) that new life has begun. The first place to begin your endeavor to overcome this

9. Richard Baxter, *Baxter's Practical Works*, vol. 1, *A Christian Directory* (Ligonier, PA: Soli Deo Gloria Publications, 1990), 357.

(or any other) life-dominating sin is to be sure that you have truly repented of your self-oriented way of living and trusted in Christ's atoning sacrifice.

Identify Your Own Specific Style of Lying

Probably your next step should be to take an inventory of your favorite deceitful maneuvers. Take a moment right now to fill out the worksheet below.

Put a check next to the specific types of lies you have been most willing to utilize.

- ☐ Outright lie (direct untruth)
- ☐ Inference (insinuation)
- ☐ Concealment
- ☐ Blame-shifting
- ☐ The "I don't know" lie
- ☐ Making commitments with no intention of keeping them
- ☐ Slandering (talebearing)
- ☐ Hidden agenda
- ☐ Fabrication
- ☐ Verbalizing suspicions or false conclusions
- ☐ Diversion
- ☐ Partial truth
- ☐ Exaggeration
- ☐ Covering up past sins
- ☐ Kidding, teasing, and joking
- ☐ Verbal and body language lies
- ☐ Claiming to be close to God while continuing in sin
- ☐ Giving the appearance of one emotion to cover up the existence of another emotion
- ☐ Planting/fabricating evidence
- ☐ Acting (e.g., pretending to be crazy)
- ☐ Other: _____
- ☐ Other: _____

Make It Your Goal to Be a "Teller of the Truth"

It is not enough for liars to stop lying. They must make it their goal to speak the truth in every situation. From the biblical perspective, the process of change always involves two factors.

There are a couple jokes that we biblical counselors sometimes tell, not because they are funny (they're actually quite corny) but because they serve as a helpful paradigm.

Here they are:

Question: When is a door not a door?

Answer: When it is ajar!

Question: When is a car not a car?

Answer: When it turns into a driveway!

A door is not a door when it becomes something else. A car is not a car when it becomes something else.

Now, when is a liar not a liar?

"When he stops lying?"

No! A liar is no longer a liar when he becomes something else—a teller of the truth.

> Therefore, laying aside falsehood, speak truth each one of you with his neighbor, for we are members of one another. (Eph. 4:25)

The two-part process of change involves putting off the wrong behavior and putting on the correct behavior. In order to put something off, we must put on something else. It is not enough to simply stop sinning. We must make it our goal to develop the corresponding positive biblical character trait as an alternative to the character deficiency we are trying to eradicate.

So, a liar will never truly stop lying if he only focuses on cutting out the lies he has been so accustomed to telling. He must rather focus on replacing the lies with the truth.

I often say to my counselees something like this: "Imagine what it will be like when some day as you walk down the street people shall say, 'There goes John. He is the most truthful, sincere person I know.'"

Now, it's probably not going to be good enough to generally be more truthful. If you really want to put off lying, you should try to figure out what the biblical alternative is to your specific style of lying.

So, what is it?

Do you *falsify* information? If so, you must make it your goal to give *accurate reports* of the information you communicate.

Is your style of lying to *conceal information*? Then, you must make it your goal to open up and *disclose* to others the information they need to know to have a proper relationship with you.

Do you *detract* from the good name of others by *slander* or *talebearing*? You must learn to be silent (to "speak evil of no man") or better yet, to use your tongue to bless others and minister grace to them.

Do you *blame others* when you are confronted with your sin? You must start *taking the hit* for your own sins! Learn the truth of the proverb that says "before honor is humility."

Of course, there are other benefits to telling the truth, not the least of which was explained by Mark Twain: "If you tell the truth, you don't have to remember anything."

I have a driving habit that really irritates my eldest daughter. I use my turn signal every time I turn the car—to change lanes, to turn around corners, when the road curves, whether or not there is someone behind me—probably even in parking lots. Pretty much, every time I have to turn the steering wheel more than a few degrees, I'm going to signal.

Not too long ago, Sophia asked me, "Daddy, why do you *always* use your turn signal?"

"Because, honey, if I always use the turn signal, I'll never get a ticket for failing to use it."

It's that way with lying: if you always tell the truth, you don't have to fear ever being caught in a lie.

Clear Your Conscience with God and with Man (Remove Guilt through Confession)

When we have lied to someone it is usually necessary to go back to that person, confess the lie, and ask for forgiveness for being deceitful. Of course, confession must first be made to God against whom all of our sins are committed.

I once had to ask my little sister, who was in her early twenties at the time, to forgive me for telling her a lie when she was a little girl. I had totally forgotten the incident, having no idea how my remarks had impacted her little life. What was this devastating lie? I told her that Smokey the Bear had died in a forest fire.

The Bible has much to say about the importance of maintaining a clear conscience.

> I myself always strive to have a conscience without offense toward God and men. (Acts 24:16 NKJV)

> But the goal of our instruction is love from a pure heart and a good conscience and a sincere faith. (1 Tim. 1:5)

> This command I entrust to you, Timothy, my son, in accordance with the prophecies previously made concerning you, that by them you fight the good fight, keeping faith and a good conscience, which some have rejected and suffered shipwreck in regard to their faith. (1 Tim. 1:18–19)

> But sanctify Christ as Lord in your hearts, always being ready to make a defense to everyone who asks you to give an account for the hope that is in you, yet with gentleness and reverence; and keep a good conscience so that in the thing in which you are slandered, those who revile your good behavior in Christ will be put to shame. (1 Peter 3:15–16)

Not only is it biblical to do so, but the humility needed to correct lies that were told in the past can also be a powerful motivation to not tell any more lies. Once a clear conscience is established, the thought of having to go back to yet another person to whom one has lied can be a powerful sanctifying force in the life of a converted liar. It is the power of a clear conscience. Richard Baxter put it well:

> When men have done that which they are afraid or ashamed to make known, they think there is a necessity of using their art to keep it secret. . . . The best way in the world to avoid lying [is] to be innocent.[10]

Notice the connection between the truth, not lying, the conscience, and the Holy Spirit in Romans 9:1.

> I am telling the *truth* in Christ, I am *not lying*, my *conscience* bearing me witness in [under the control of] the *Holy Spirit.*

Paul calls his conscience (which has been sanctified by the Holy Spirit) as witness that he was not lying. Is your conscience under the Spirit's control? If you hope to learn how to stop lying, it needs to be. But it can't be if you are grieving Him (cf. Eph. 4:30) by not dealing biblically with your guilt.

Be Willing to Earn Back the Trust You May Have Lost from Those to Whom You Have Lied

Nothing causes others to lose trust in us more quickly than telling a lie. In fact, in the dozens of marital infidelity cases I've had the privilege to work with, the faithful partners invariably found it more difficult to believe that their spouses would never lie again than they would to believe that their spouses would never be unfaithful again. In the final analysis, the lying was usually a more difficult and lengthier obstacle for the faithful spouses to "put behind them" than

10. Ibid.

the infidelity. This is especially true when the adulterous affair went on for more than a few weeks.

There is a distinction between forgiveness and trust. They are not the same thing. If I sin against you and ask for your forgiveness, it is incumbent upon you as a Christian to forgive me (Matt. 18:21–35; Luke 17:3–10). You must essentially take the hurt I have caused you, wrap it up in a pretty package, put a bow on it, and present it back to me on a silver platter. It is not, however, incumbent upon you to also place on that silver platter the trust I may have lost as a result of my sin. Rather, it is incumbent upon me to earn back the trust I have lost as a result of my sin.

The key to earning back trust that has been lost is to habitually do the opposite of what was done to lose it. So, if you lost trust as a result of falsifying information, you must make it your goal to earn (win back) the trust you relinquished by accurately reporting future events. If trust was lost as a result of your concealing information, you will have to earn trust by revealing things that your hearers have a biblical need to know. In fact, I have told countless counselees, "The next time your spouse or parents ask you a question, give them more information than they could possibly assimilate. The idea is to give them so much relevant and detailed information that they think to themselves (if not say to you), 'I'm sorry I asked . . . thanks, but I really don't need that much information; I believe you already!'"

Identify and Dethrone Idolatrous Lusts and Replace Their Corresponding Fears with the Fear of the Lord

The case can be made that some form of fear motivates virtually every lie (i.e., fear of being found out, fear of embarrassment, fear of being punished). There are usually two sides to idolatrous desires: one side that inordinately desires something and another that inordinately fears losing that same something. It is often helpful to explore what it is you are wanting or are afraid of losing so much that you are willing to lie. *A lover of*

29

money may lie to gain wealth (or to keep from losing it). A person *who loves the approval of man* may lie to get others to like him or to avoid being hurt or rejected (or even having a conflict). A *child who loves pleasure* may lie about his homework out of fear that he will not have enough time to play if he tells the truth.

If you want to stop lying, you must learn to fear God more than you fear anything else. You must trust the Lord to protect you from that which you fear, and to provide you with all the necessary grace should that which you fear come upon you.

Although *fear* is by far the greatest motive behind deception, there are other reasons why people lie. R. C. Sproul offers us a few more:

> Why do people lie to and about each other? Why, for that matter, did Satan . . . lie to Eve in the garden? Partly from malice, partly from pride. When you lie to do someone wrong, it is malice; when you lie to impress, move, and use him, and to keep him from seeing you in a bad light, it is pride. . . . Fear, contempt, and revenge, boastful conceit, fraud, and the desire to shine by telling a good story are other motives which prompt lies.[11]

Here's the bottom line: When we lie, it is because we don't trust God to meet our needs! Perhaps the greatest desire that tempts most of us to lie is the desire for the approval of others. Richard Baxter also has some good advice on this matter.

> If you would not be a liar, get over your pride and inordinate concern for the opinions of men. Pride makes men *so* desirous of reputation, and so impatient of the hard opinions of others, that all the honest endeavors of the proud are too little to produce the reputation they desire, and therefore lying must make up the rest. Shame is so intolerant a suffering for them, that they make lies the familiar cover of their nakedness. He who has pride but has not riches, and longs to be thought of as somebody, will show off his estate by a lie. He who has not

11. Packer, *Growing in Christ*, 272.

eminency of parentage and birth, if he be proud, will make himself a gentleman by a lie. . . . He who lacks education or degrees or anything that he would be proud of, will endeavor by a lie to supply what he lacks. . . . But if your pride were cured, your temptation to lie would be as nothing. You would be so indifferent to matters of honor or reputation as to not venture your souls on God's displeasure for it.[12]

Find Someone to Help Hold You Accountable for Telling the Truth

Do you remember what Peter did after he denied the Lord (lied) three times?

"He wept bitterly."

That's right. But do you remember what happened between his last lie and his first tear? Check it out:

> Having arrested Him, they led Him away and brought Him to the house of the high priest; but Peter was following at a distance. After they had kindled a fire in the middle of the courtyard and had sat down together, Peter was sitting among them. And a servant-girl, seeing him as he sat in the firelight and looking intently at him, said, "This man was with Him too." But he denied it, saying, "Woman, I do not know Him." [Lie 1] A little later, another saw him and said, "You are one of them too!" But Peter said, "Man, I am not!" [Lie 2] After about an hour had passed, another man began to insist, saying, "Certainly this man also was with Him, for he is a Galilean too." But Peter said, "Man, I do not know what you are talking about." [Lie 3] Immediately, while he was still speaking, a rooster crowed. *The Lord turned and looked at Peter.* And Peter remembered the word of the Lord, how He had told him, "Before a rooster crows today, you will deny Me three times." And he went out and wept bitterly. (Luke 22:54–62)

Just one look from the Lord was all it took to reduce Peter to tears. That's the power of accountability. When we struggle with habitual sin patterns, we sometimes need others to come

12. Baxter, *Christian Directory*, 357.

alongside of us to help us obey God's Word. Sometimes, those I counsel know exactly what God expects them to do to change— and have known for years. What counseling provided was not so much new information, but rather the motivation that account- ability provides. If you are accountable only to yourself in this life, you have only yourself to answer to. But if you are account- able to others in this life, you will have less to give an account for in the next!

Now you know how to experience the joy of a clear con- science and the honor that comes from having the reputation of being a man or woman of integrity. May the Lord grant you the wisdom and the strength both to put off lying and to increas- ingly become a "teller of the truth!"